MARSDEN HARTLEY
Painting, Number 5. 1914-15.
Oil. 39½ x 31¾.

Whitney Museum of American Art,
anonymous gift.

PIONEERS
OF MODERN ART
IN AMERICA

THE DECADE OF THE ARMORY SHOW, 1910-1920

BY LLOYD GOODRICH

PUBLISHED FOR THE WHITNEY MUSEUM OF AMERICAN ART
BY FREDERICK A. PRAEGER, PUBLISHERS, NEW YORK, 1963

BOOKS THAT MATTER

Published in the United States of America in 1963
by Frederick A. Praeger, Inc., Publisher
64 University Place, New York 3, N. Y.
LIBRARY OF CONGRESS CATALOGUE
CARD NUMBER 63-13597

FOREWORD

The Armory Show of 1913 was a landmark in American art — the first large-scale introduction of modern art to the people of the United States. No single event, before or since, has had such an impact on the art world of this country. This year is the fiftieth anniversary of the famous exhibition.

For the last five years the Friends of the Whitney Museum of American Art have staged annual loan exhibitions, in collaboration with the staff of the Museum. This year the Friends' Exhibitions Committee felt that the most appropriate offering should be an exhibition commemorating the historic anniversary of the Armory Show. The plan seemed especially fitting because the interests and activities of the Friends, like those of the Whitney Museum, are devoted primarily to twentieth-century American art, in which the Armory Show played so decisive a role.

The Committee agreed that no attempt should be made to reconstruct the original Armory Show, a project which was being ably and thoroughly carried out by the Munson-Williams-Proctor Institute of Utica, in a large exhibition to be seen later in the old 69th Regiment Armory in New York. Since the most history-making feature of the 1913 event was the foreign section, it seemed inappropriate for an association concerned with American art to base its exhibition on the actual Armory Show. Rather, the Committee decided to present a survey of the advanced art of the United States during the decade of 1910 to 1920. It was agreed not to limit this survey to the artists who were represented in the 1913 show; indeed, the survey was broadened to include Americans who were living in Europe at the time. The aim has been to picture in comprehensive terms the growth of American modern art in the critical and fruitful decade of which the Armory Show was the outstanding event.

On behalf of the Friends of the Whitney Museum I want to extend most sincere thanks to the members of the Exhibitions Committee, who gave generously of their time and knowledge in planning the exhibition. I also want to express our appreciation to Lloyd Goodrich for his hospitality to the ideas of the Committee and his patience with the Committee's personal preferences in the selection of the artists and works to be included. Special thanks go to the Whitney Museum staff, and in particular to Edward Bryant, Associate Curator, who devoted uncounted hours and labor to the complex research involved in uncovering works of the decade and in securing them for the exhibition.

HERBERT M. ROTHSCHILD
Chairman, Exhibitions Committee, Friends of the Whitney Museum of American Art

EXHIBITIONS COMMITTEE (1962-1963)

Herbert M. Rothschild, *Chairman*
Lawrence H. Bloedel
Irving Mitchell Felt
Mrs. Alfred L. Loomis
Stanley A. Marks
Miss Patricia V. Marx
David A. Prager

1 American art in the first decade of our century was the mirror of a society that was prosperous and seemingly secure. In these years before the First World War, all things seemed for the best in this best of worlds. True, there were a few disquieting phenomena such as Votes for Women, the hobble skirt, the new dancing craze; but to the United States of 1900 to 1914, today's America would have seemed unbelievable.

The American art world was at peace. The few surviving nineteenth-century leaders — Homer, La Farge, Eakins, Ryder — were nearing the end of their creative activity. The current leaders, mostly products of the academic schools abroad, had settled comfortably into the limited tradition of the salons. The last international movement to reach these shores had been impressionism, which had combined with native idealism and sentiment to produce an art devoted to the smiling aspects of life, to family and home, to the idyllic in nature, and to the virtues and wholesomeness of American womanhood.

This academic art had its own merits: technical skill, sound draftsmanship, refinements of color and tone, pleasure in handling the brush. Its basic limitation was its belief that painting and sculpture were primarily naturalistic representation. There might be different modes of representation: the impressionists' preoccupation with outdoor light and atmosphere, the Sargent school's striving for photographic verisimilitude and brilliant brushwork, the tasteful decorativeness of Whistler's followers. But all were concerned with visual appearances, technical skill, and taste, rather than with the more essential elements of form and design.

The academic world was quite oblivious to what had been going on abroad since impressionism. In France, Cézanne, Gauguin, Van Gogh and Seurat, rejecting impressionism's concentration on visual phenomena, had re-created reality in terms of fundamental form. Now, in the opening decade of the century, Matisse and the men around him — Derain, Braque, Vlaminck, Rouault — were carrying these innovations much further, using nature only as a starting-point for painting in which color, line and pattern spoke with a direct physical impact. Figures and objects, drastically distorted, were translated into powerful rhythmic patterns; color was raised to a new purity and intensity. In the Salon d'Automne of 1905 the group, appearing in full strength, created a public reaction as violent as the impressionists' debut thirty years earlier, and were dubbed *"les fauves"* — the wild beasts.

In this same Autumn Salon appeared ten paintings by Cézanne, last survivor of the post-impressionists, still little known. Ten more canvases were shown in 1906, the year he died, and next fall came the great memorial exhibition. For the younger painters Cézanne's concern with sculptural form began to outweigh Gauguin's primitivism and Van Gogh's expressionism. In 1907 Picasso commenced *Les Demoiselles d'Avignon,* and within a year cubism had been born. In contrast to fauvism's emphasis on color, line and pattern, cubism was an exploration of three-dimensional volumes. The object was broken down into its geometric components, reassembled in new combinations, pictured from different sides simultaneously. At first subject matter was confined to concrete objects, and color was secondary and monochromatic; but in a few years this severe "analytical" phase flowered into the free inventions of synthetic cubism. In the meantime, cubism's radical transformations had given birth to other innovations, including the beginnings of pure abstraction. Paris became the center of new movements, crowding one upon another, that changed the basic concepts of art throughout the Western world.

In these developments more than a score of Americans participated. As early as the 1890's Maurice Prendergast had discovered Cézanne and Bonnard,

LYONEL FEININGER

Old American Locomotive.
1910. Oil. 19¾ x 39½.

Collection of Mrs. Lyonel Feininger.

MAURICE PRENDERGAST
The Balloon. 1910. Watercolor. 13½ x 19½.
Addison Gallery of American Art.

MARGUERITE ZORACH
Provincetown — Moonset and Sunrise.
1916. Oil. 20 x 24.

Kraushaar Galleries.

and had begun to evolve his highly personal lyrical and decorative art, whose growing freedom paralleled fauvism. He can be called the first American modernist — the first to paint pictures which, using nature only for motifs, were independent creations in color and rhythmic pattern.

After the turn of the century more young Americans arrived in Paris and came in contact with modernism: Alfred Maurer (who had come in 1897), Karfiol in 1901, Halpert in 1902, Sterne in 1904. From 1905 the numbers increased: in that year, Marin and Weber; in 1905 or 1906, Russell and Bruce; in 1906, Walkowitz; in 1907, Dove, Carles, Pach, Macdonald-Wright, Demuth and Marguerite Zorach; in 1908, Covert, Benton, Schamberg and Storrs; in 1909, Sheeler and Dasburg; in 1910, William Zorach and Preston Dickinson. Never before had so many Americans been involved so early in an international movement.

Mostly in their early or middle twenties, they had seen little or no modern art back home. Their first contact with it came in the fauve showings at the Autumn Salons, where they also discovered Cézanne. Usually they had entered the academic schools, but on becoming aware of what was going on, they struck out for themselves. In time, they met Matisse and Picasso and the other Parisian leaders. Weber became a close friend of the Douanier Rousseau, whose genius he was one of the first to recognize, at a time when the French critics still considered him a harmless lunatic. Rousseau, who was far from a modernist, was worried by his young friend's advanced tendencies, and his parting words when Weber left Paris were, *"N'oubliez pas la nature, Weber."*

Their education in modernism was helped by four Americans living in Paris, the Steins — Leo, Gertrude, Michael, and the latter's wife Sarah — the first serious collectors of Matisse, Picasso and other contemporaries. Leo and Gertrude Stein's collection became such a Mecca for the modern-minded that they started their Saturday evening receptions, where one could not only see the pictures but meet the painters. In 1908 the Michael Steins and a few others, including Weber and Bruce, induced Matisse to start his famous class, which eventually included several other Americans. A French paper, making fun of the class, asked, "Where do these people come from?" and answered, "From Massachusetts."

To most of the Americans modern art was bewildering at first, and they did not at once embrace it. For almost all, Cézanne was the first and most lasting influence. Matisse and the fauves were more comprehensible than Picasso and the cubists. Their own work abroad was seldom radical. They were still followers,

MAURICE STERNE

Dance of the Elements, Bali. 1913. Oil. 57 x 65.

The North Carolina Museum of Art.

OSCAR BLUEMNER
Old Canal Port. 1914. Oil. 30¼ x 40¼.

Whitney Museum of American Art.

SAMUEL HALPERT
Brooklyn Bridge. 1913. Oil. 34 x 42.

Whitney Museum of American Art,
gift of Mr. and Mrs. Benjamin Halpert.

JOHN MARIN
Landscape in Maine. 1915. Watercolor. 16½ x 18½.

The Art Institute of Chicago.

ABRAHAM WALKOWITZ
New York. 1917. Watercolor, ink and pencil. 30⅝ x 21¾.

Whitney Museum of American Art, gift of the artist in memory of Juliana Force.

not in the vanguard. Only after returning to the United States did most of them develop more advanced styles. Nevertheless they were more *au courant* than any of their predecessors abroad, and they brought back ideas that were revolutionary in this country.

Their relations to the European movements were as diverse as they were. Karfiol's sensual, tender poetry was less close to the fauves than to the post-impressionists Cézanne and the later Renoir. Halpert's bold patterns and massive modeling related him to the fauves, especially early Derain. Maurer and Carles became converts to fauvism, painting exuberant landscapes à la Matisse before developing their mature individual styles. Also fauvist was Weber's work immediately after his return to America: idyllic figure compositions, luxuriant in form and color, with a full-blooded sensuousness that made academic American painting seem anemic. Others related to fauvism at some period were Bruce, Walkowitz, Demuth, and Marguerite and William Zorach.

A few Americans developed outside the Parisian scene. Stella's relations were with Italian futurism, Hartley's with the Munich *Blaue Reiter* group of expressionists. The German-born Oscar Bluemner, revisiting his native land in mature years, was akin to German expressionism in his fantasy and his emphatic linear patterns and deep violent color. Konrad Cramer, also German by birth, was in touch with the Munich group before coming to America in 1911. Sterne, a lover of both ancient and modern art, after years in Paris embarked on a four-year voyage to the Orient, ending with two years in Bali. In his Bali paintings tropical life was pictured in a style essentially classic, combining representation with strong geometric design related to the cubists and Duchamp.

Some Americans lived abroad for years and became integral members of the European art world. Lyonel Feininger, born and brought up in New York, at sixteen (in 1887) went to Germany and became a leader of European modernism, returning to this country in his sixties. Albert Bloch, also American-born, lived in Germany from 1908 to 1921 and exhibited with *Der Blaue Reiter* and *Der Sturm*. Maurer returned from Paris to the United States only in 1914, Bruce in the 1930's. Two Americans in Paris, Russell and Macdonald-Wright, started a movement of their own, Synchromism.

On the other hand, some future modernists spent years abroad without being affected by or even aware of the new movements. John Marin, a complete individualist, was little influenced by his five years in Europe, 1905 to 1910, and his first real introduction to modern art came through Alfred Stieglitz after his return. The same seems to have been true of Arthur Dove. John Covert, back in America

MAURICE PRENDERGAST

The Promenade. 1913. Oil. 30 x 34.

Whitney Museum of American Art, bequest of Alexander M. Bing.

JOHN MARIN

Woolworth Building in Construction. 1913. Watercolor. 19 x 15¼.

Collection of Mr. and Mrs. John C. Marin, Jr.

after six years of conventional study and work in Munich and Paris, suddenly began to produce his highly original semi-abstract inventions — only to abandon painting, as suddenly, eight years later.

Other modernists did not go abroad until the 1920's — Man Ray, Burlin, McFee, Stuart Davis. These men became acquainted with modern art as it could be found in the United States, through books and magazines, infrequent exhibitions, and the Armory Show. For Burlin, the Show's revelation was confirmed by Southwest Indian art during seven years in New Mexico. There were at least two cases of purely spontaneous modernism, without discernible influence: Georgia O'Keeffe's and Charles Burchfield's early pictures. But with few exceptions it was European — and usually French — modernism that furnished the initial stimulus.

2 When the modernists came home from Europe in the 1900's they found a very different artistic climate. The United States' phenomenal material growth had not been matched by artistic growth. The art world was completely conservative. For us today it is hard to realize conditions fifty years ago. The few dealers interested in American art were committed to the academicians. For a young or unknown artist, the only way to reach the public was through the big annual exhibitions of museums and artists' societies, controlled by conservative juries who excluded the non-conformist. Acceptance or rejection by these shows could mean artistic survival or failure. Prizes, conveying a false prestige, went to fellow members of the academic fold. Museums were concerned with the past, or if with the present, only with the safely conservative. In 1908, the year of "The Eight" show and Stieglitz's first modern exhibitions, the then director of the Metropolitan Museum, Sir Caspar Purdon Clark, declared publicly: "There is a state of unrest all over the world in art as in all other things. It is the same in literature as in music, in painting and in sculpture, and I dislike unrest." The critics, with few exceptions, were uncomprehending or hostile. Under such conditions, a non-academic artist found it almost impossible to exhibit or sell his work.

One artist group, however, was fighting academic domination — "The Eight." Its nucleus was five realist painters, all Philadelphians, all ex-newspaper artists, all close friends: Robert Henri (the oldest and the leader), George Luks, William Glackens, John Sloan and Everett Shinn. In revolt against academic idealism they were picturing the contemporary life of America, particularly city life. Far from radical in style, they belonged in the naturalistic tradition of Velázquez, Goya, Daumier, and the pre-impressionist Manet. But their subject matter made them

MARCEL DUCHAMP
Nude Descending a Staircase, No. 3. 1916.
Watercolor, ink, crayon and
pastel over photographic base. 58 x 35½.

Philadelphia Museum of Art,
The Louise and Walter Arensberg Collection.

ARTHUR B. DAVIES
Intermezzo. c.1915. Oil. 28 x 14.

Graham Gallery.

ARTHUR B. DAVIES
Interformed. c.1915. Oil. 20 x 14.

Graham Gallery.

seem radical to the established art world, which labelled them "Apostles of Ugliness" and "The Black Gang."

Shortly after 1900, when all the group had moved to New York, they began their battle with the academy. Soon they became allied with three other painters, of different viewpoints but similar liberal beliefs: the pioneer modernist Maurice Prendergast, the impressionist Ernest Lawson, and the romantic traditionalist Arthur B. Davies. Beginning in 1904 the group organized a series of exhibitions, the most famous of which was "The Eight" show at the Macbeth Gallery in 1908, which aroused wide public interest and controversy — a show that had an effect out of proportion to its size. Although they never again exhibited together as a group, individual members, particularly Henri, Sloan and Davies, continued to lead the fight for independent art. In 1910, with Walt Kuhn and others, they staged their most ambitious demonstration so far, a big no-jury exhibition in a rented building on West 35th Street: a miscellaneous show, prevailingly liberal, including few modernists. In many respects this was the prototype of the American section of the Armory Show. The following year Henri's ex-student Rockwell Kent initiated another independent show, which produced the first split in the Eight, with Davies, Prendergast and Luks joining nine other artists, including the modernists Marin, Maurer and Hartley. From this time on, Davies, the one continuing leader, allied himself more and more with the modernists.

In these years the only gallery in America that consistently exhibited modern art was Alfred Stieglitz's little Photo-Secession Gallery at 291 Fifth Avenue, which began showing painting and sculpture in 1908. A pioneer photographer and a champion of the new in every field; a bold incisive mind, intolerant of the stupid and dead; a magnetic personality, attracting gifted disciples; and a fighter who delighted in battling against heavy odds, Stieglitz conducted his campaign for modern art with brilliancy and corrosive humor. He had able collaborators, especially Edward Steichen, painter and fellow photographer, then living in France, and Marius de Zayas, Mexican-born caricaturist, a highly sophisticated world citizen.

Stieglitz's gallery was small, in a shabby building with a creaking elevator, but as Hartley said, "It was probably the largest small room of its kind in the world." The list of Stieglitz "firsts" is still impressive: among others, the first exhibitions in America of Matisse, Rousseau, Cézanne, Picasso, Picabia, Brancusi, and African Negro sculpture. But Stieglitz also believed passionately in the future of American art, and specifically in certain young modernists. He was the first to give one-man shows to Maurer, Marin, Hartley, Dove, Carles, Bluemner, Nadelman, O'Keeffe and Macdonald-Wright. His "Younger American Artists" exhibition

WALT KUHN
Girl in White Chemise. c.1920. Oil. 30 x 25.

Walt Kuhn Estate.

WALTER PACH
St. Patrick's at Night. 1916. Oil. 18½ x 24½.

Collection of Mrs. Walter Pach.

JULES PASCIN
La Belle Californienne. 1917. Oil. 35 x 27.

Collection of Paul Josefowitz.

in 1910 was probably the first all-modern group show. The foreign things he exhibited, while not all "important," were always examples of the most advanced work being done abroad. He himself described 291 as a "laboratory." Here the modernists could meet, and with Stieglitz as a catalyst, engage in that endless talk that is the essential accompaniment of any new movement. Stieglitz also published a quarterly, *Camera Work*, much broader than its title, the most radical American magazine of arts and letters.

It can be imagined how the public and critics, who had considered Glackens and Sloan "Apostles of Ugliness," reacted to the kind of art shown at 291. It was here that the perennial remark, "My seven-year-old child can draw better," was first heard. Newspaper criticism ranged from indifference through bewilderment and derision to abuse. Of the Weber show in 1911 one reviewer wrote, "It is difficult to write about these atrocities with moderation," while another called it "a brutal, vulgar and unnecessary display of art license." Stieglitz diabolically reprinted these imbecilities in *Camera Work,* where they remain embalmed for posterity.

Thus 291 became a focus for the new forces, exercising a unique influence on the avant-garde of the day. But the larger public had still been given little opportunity to see European modernism. This opportunity was to be furnished by the Armory Show.

3 In its inception the Armory Show was a continuation of the independent American exhibitions in which the Eight had played such a part. Its growth into something much bigger has been described by several participants, notably by Walt Kuhn in his 1938 pamphlet, *The Story of the Armory Show.* The project was conceived in 1911 in the Madison Gallery, an enterprise devoted to showing younger artists, conducted by Mrs. Clara Potter Davidge and supported largely by Gertrude Vanderbilt Whitney. Here three artists who were having an exhibition, Kuhn, Jerome Myers and Elmer MacRae, and the gallery's director, Henry Fitch Taylor, "would sit and talk about the helplessness of our situation," as Kuhn said. Finally in December 1911 they decided to do something about it, and invited additional artists to join the discussions. By early January the group grew to twenty-five members, calling themselves the Association of American Painters and Sculptors. It included all the Eight except Shinn, younger independents such as Bellows and Du Bois, and others of varying degrees of liberalism. In general they were not modernists but believers in the independent idea; the Stieglitz group was conspicuously absent, and the only one whose current work could be called mod-

CHARLES DEMUTH

The Circus. 1917. Watercolor. 8 x 10⅝.

The Columbus Gallery of Fine Arts, Ferdinand Howald Collection.

ern was the veteran Prendergast. It is paradoxical that this, the most important event in the history of American modernism, was not staged by modernists. It is also noteworthy that it was organized entirely by artists — not by museums, art patrons or dealers.

The initial plan was for a big independent show, without juries or prizes, including a few things from abroad. But after Davies was elected president the project became transformed. In his own art Davies might be a romantic visionary, but he was also a sophisticated mind, fully aware of the modern movements, here and abroad. He was a frequent visitor at 291, and had bought two Webers from the painter's first one-man show in 1909. Beneath a quiet, retiring exterior, he possessed unexpected energy and practicality, and an iron will. (He also had the valuable gift of interesting the wealthy in the new art.) Many of the Association were still thinking in terms of another American exhibition, but Davies believed that what America needed was a firsthand view of European modern art.

In the fall of 1912 Davies, receiving a catalogue of the large Sonderbund exhibition in Cologne, sent it to Kuhn, the Association's secretary, with a note, "I wish we could have a show like this." Kuhn's answer was to take ship for Europe, arriving in Cologne the last day of the show. The Sonderbund exhibition

CHARLES BURCHFIELD
Snowstorm in the Woods. 1917.
Watercolor and gouache. 20⅛ x 42⅛.

The Art Institute of Chicago.

CHARLES BURCHFIELD

Church Bells Ringing, Rainy Winter Night. 1917. Watercolor. 30 x 19.

The Cleveland Museum of Art, gift of Mrs. Louise M. Dunn, in memory of Henry G. Keller.

with its representation of Van Gogh, Cézanne and Gauguin became the model for the New York show (though few of the same works were included). After visiting The Hague, Munich and Berlin, Kuhn arrived in Paris, where he looked up Walter Pach, who had been living there for several years and knew all the avant-garde artists and galleries. Pach's help proved invaluable. Davies was cabled to join them, and for a week or so the three lived in cabs, visiting artists and persuading them to let America see their work — among others, Marcel Duchamp, whose recent paintings Kuhn rightly felt would be the sensation of the show. Dealers were at first less amenable; why withdraw their pictures from the European market for six months without a chance of sales? But in the end they cooperated. After Davies and Kuhn returned to America, Pach as the Association's European agent superintended the assembling and shipping.

Working on a shoestring, the Association had leased the huge 69th Regiment Armory at Lexington Avenue and 25th Street, at $5,500 for a month. Everyone who could help was pressed into service. Kuhn's friend John Quinn donated his legal aid. Frederick James Gregg, a newspaperman and critic, helped with publicity, as did Du Bois, who edited (and ghost-wrote) a whole issue of *Arts and Decoration* devoted to the show. The public's curiosity was aroused by news stories; few events except the circus had better advance publicity. The Association adopted a motto, "The New Spirit," and an emblem, the pinetree flag of Massachusetts during the American Revolution; and buttons bearing these two were distributed by the thousands.

The Association was deluged with applications from American artists, and a committee headed by Glackens coped with this problem. Because he and Davies wanted a fine big show, works continued to be accepted even after it opened, and Allen Tucker, in charge of the catalogue, had a hopeless task; although the catalogue and its supplement list 1090 works by 306 artists, actually several hundred more were hung. As Kuhn said, "It was bedlam — but we liked it." The problem of turning a big open floor-space into galleries was solved, after lengthy discussion, by Bellows. Mrs. Whitney gave a thousand dollars for greenery and decorations. The treasury was chronically empty, but Davies performed miracles of producing funds when needed. No artist member of the Association was asked to contribute a penny, nor did any of those who helped receive a cent.

The International Exhibition of Modern Art, as it was officially called, opened with a gala reception on February 17, 1913. It was the most remarkable piece of artistic showmanship so far presented in this country. Its most novel and startling feature for Americans was the foreign section. As a survey of modern art in Paris, from the full representation of Cézanne, Gauguin and Van Gogh to the latest word, it has seldom been equalled. On the other hand, the German, Italian and English

BERNARD KARFIOL
Boy Bathers. 1916. Oil. 28 x 36.

Whitney Museum of American Art.

ANDREW DASBURG
Portrait of Judson Smith. c.1923. Oil. 29⅞ x 24.

Dallas Museum of Fine Arts.

moderns were almost completely absent. Gregg blithely explained that the organizers had found that "most of the German Post-Impressionists were adapters, the result being that very little of what they had done had any real significance" — an attitude that persisted in America for many years. The Italian futurists had been urged to participate by Davies, Kuhn and Pach in Paris, but as they insisted on separate galleries with their own box office, they were omitted.

The American section, about two-thirds of the whole, was a great comprehensive hodgepodge, ranging from stray academicians to modernists, with the latter a small minority, and mild progressives in the majority. Among modernists there were some absences, for one reason or another: Weber, Sterne, Feininger, Dove, Macdonald-Wright, Demuth. (Weber was showing in the Grafton Gallery in London, Sterne was in Bali, etc.). But on the whole it was an accurate reflection of the state of non-academic art in this country. This was the first opportunity for American independents to take stock of themselves in comparison with the European vanguard, and their reaction was not self-congratulatory. Even Gregg wrote that "the vast mass of the American works exhibited represented simply arrested development." Glackens said: "We have no innovators here. Everything worth while in our art is due to the influence of French art," but he added: "There is promise of a renaissance in American art."

But it was the foreign section that contained the dynamite — especially the fauves and cubists. The public was bewildered, shocked, but enormously curious. The cubist rooms were always jammed, and the crowd around Duchamp's *Nude Descending a Staircase* was so thick that one had to wait one's turn. The show became a main topic of conversation, and visiting it a social necessity. Families were divided, friendships broken. "Cubist" jokes filled the newspapers and magazines (also jokes about "futurists," though there were none). Attendance, slow at first, mounted steadily as word got around, reaching about 10,000 on the closing day. Probably about 75,000 saw the show in New York. Walter Pach, in charge of the sales staff, also wrote pamphlets, lectured, answered questions, and countered jeering or insulting comments.

After closing in New York the exhibition went to the Art Institute of Chicago, including most of the foreign section and a selection of American works — a total of about 500. The public reception was even more violent; the Institute's students, egged on by their more conservative instructors, burnt Matisse and Brancusi — and even poor Pach — in effigy. The attendance, stimulated partly by rumors of immorality, was more than double that in New York. Thence the show minus its Americans moved to Copley Hall, Boston, where it was given a cold shoulder by

MAX WEBER

The Visit. 1919. Oil. 40 x 30.

Collection of Mr. and Mrs. Milton Lowenthal.

artists and respectable society. Probably about 300,000 people saw it altogether. About 150 paintings and sculptures, mostly foreign, had been sold.

The show had its defenders in the press, but the regular critics were almost all violently opposed. "Madmen," "charlatans," "poseurs," "artistic anarchists" were the usual epithets. "This is not a movement," wrote Royal Cortissoz. "It is unadulterated cheek." Theodore Roosevelt, turned art critic for *The Outlook*, called the cubists "a lunatic fringe." One of the most solid reviews on either side was that of Kenyon Cox, written with the logic that made him a leader of the conservatives. Cox was not bewildered, like his colleagues; he saw clearly what modernism meant — the antithesis of the old American school. His statement, "The real meaning of this cubist movement is the total destruction of the art of painting," needs only the addition of "as practised by my generation" to be an accurate declaration of modernist aims. No less true is his accusation, "The artist is no longer to occupy himself with the problem of how things look — he is interested only in how he feels about things." His article, better thought-out and expressed than most, is still worth reading as a revelation of the old America faced with the new.

But for the pioneer modernists who had been bearing the brunt of the battle, the moral effect was decisive. They still had hard years ahead, but they would never again feel so defenseless. Even those who had lived in Paris could learn from such startling new developments as Duchamp's *Nude*. And a whole younger generation had its first introduction to modern art in the show; as Stuart Davis has said, "The Armory Show was the greatest single influence I have experienced in all my work." Speaking for myself, as one who visited the show several times in my pre-art-student days, I can testify to its impact. To one brought up on the old masters and American impressionism, here was the revelation of a whole new world of art, alive with a freshness, a direct physical power, a vitality and delight, beyond anything I had ever seen or felt.

4 No international movement had ever before been launched in America in this way. Stieglitz had been a trail-blazer; but the Armory Show was the first full-scale introduction of modern art to the public and to most artists. With it modernism in full force burst upon the nation. In the past there had been a time-lag of fifteen or twenty years before European movements — even the latest, impressionism — had reached us. But within eight years of the emergence of fauvism and five years of that of cubism, the Armory Show presented a panorama of current developments in Paris. No single event, before or since, has had such an influence

WILLIAM ZORACH

Yosemite Falls. 1920. Oil. 72 x 30.

The Downtown Gallery.

WILLIAM ZORACH

Leo Ornstein — Piano Concert. 1918. Oil. 30 x 24.

The Downtown Gallery.

KONRAD CRAMER

Improvisation Number 2. 1913. Oil. 28 x 24.

Estate of Konrad Cramer.

MARSDEN HARTLEY
Movement Number 2. 1916. Oil. 23¼ x 19¼ (sight).

Wadsworth Atheneum, Hartford.

on American art. Doubtless modernism would have had its effect in the end, but the process was enormously accelerated by the show.

In the next few years the whole battlefield broadened, the participants multiplied. Galleries began to follow the lead of 291. N. E. Montross, an old-time dealer who had remained young in spirit, put on a series of modern shows selected by Davies. New galleries appeared, such as Marius de Zayas' Modern Gallery, Stephan Bourgeois' gallery, where Pach helped to show the moderns, and Charles Daniel, who for years was to launch young Americans. The art patron and critic Hamilton Easter Field turned part of his old house on Columbia Heights, Brooklyn, into an art gallery where younger artists were shown.

Gertrude Vanderbilt Whitney, friend of Henri and Davies and other liberals, in 1914 opened the Whitney Studio, directed by her dynamic new assistant Juliana Force. The following year Mrs. Whitney formed the Friends of the Young Artists, dedicated to the independent principle of "No juries, no prizes." Out of this in 1918 grew the Whitney Studio Club, with Mrs. Force as director, devoted to exhibiting, purchasing and selling the works of younger and liberal artists — soon the liveliest center of progressive American art in the country.

The long fight for an open salon without juries or prizes culminated in the founding in 1916 of the Society of Independent Artists. Its organizers were more modernist than those of the Armory Show: Walter Pach was the central figure, with the advice of Marcel Duchamp, Albert Gleizes and Walter Conrad Arensberg. It was patterned on the thirty-two-year-old Paris Indépendants, which had showed Cézanne, Van Gogh, Seurat, Matisse and Derain when official salons were closed to them. At the same time, it was the logical carrying-out of the principles for which the American liberals had always fought. Glackens was its first president, succeeded next year and thereafter by Sloan. It was a completely democratic artists' organization: anyone who subscribed to its platform and paid his five dollars was a voting member and could exhibit. Democracy was carried even further than in Paris by hanging all entries alphabetically — Duchamp's idea. The Independent was an assurance that no artist should be denied the right to reach the public; as Sloan said, it "kept an open door in American art." Its annual spring show became the big democratic festival of the art season, including its share of cranks and amateurs but also many new talents.

During the World War several European modernists came to live in the United States: Duchamp, Gleizes, Francis Picabia. This new phenomenon, a sign of America's entrance into the world art community, was the beginning of a westward movement which has increasingly enriched the creative life of this country.

STUART DAVIS

Boats, Gloucester. 1917. Oil. 18½ x 22¼.

Collection of Mrs. Edith Gregor Halpert.

ARTHUR G. DOVE
Team of Horses. 1911. Pastel. 17 x 21.

Collection of Dr. Mary B. Holt.

ARTHUR G. DOVE
Pagan Philosophy. 1913. Pastel. 21⅜ x 17⅞.

The Metropolitan Museum of Art, The Alfred Stieglitz Collection, 1949.

In particular Duchamp, equally at home in Paris and New York, and today an American citizen, acted as leaven in the rising modern movement.

American collecting of modern art, almost nil before 1913, really began with the Armory Show. Arensberg bought Duchamp's *Nude* (though not from the show), commissioned the artist to paint another version over a photographic base, and formed his remarkable advanced collection, now in the Philadelphia Museum of Art. John Quinn with Kuhn's and Pach's advice assembled one of the world's most comprehensive modern collections. Miss Lillie P. Bliss with Davies' help collected with fine discrimination. Other early modern collectors were Arthur Jerome Eddy of Chicago, and Albert C. Barnes. In Washington, Duncan Phillips in 1918 established the Phillips Memorial Gallery, the country's first public gallery devoted chiefly to living art, including a large proportion of Americans. In 1920 Katherine S. Dreier in collaboration with Duchamp and Man Ray founded the Société Anonyme, to promote the understanding of modern art through exhibitions, lectures and publications. The Société's collection, formed over the years by Miss Dreier and Duchamp, and now in the Yale University Art Gallery, was notable for its emphasis on the most advanced trends and on international movements not confined to the School of Paris.

Museums still brought up the rear. Although the Metropolitan through its curator of paintings Bryson Burroughs had purchased from the Armory Show Cézanne's *Colline des Pauvres* (his first work to enter a public collection in this country), it was years before American museums accepted the validity of modern art. Almost the only exception was the Newark Museum, under its progressive director John Cotton Dana, whose Max Weber exhibition in 1913 was probably the first one-man show of an American modernist in an American museum.

New magazines appeared (often short-lived) devoted to modern art and letters: *The Soil, The Little Review, The Seven Arts;* while the venerable *Dial,* with a new lease on life, published Henry McBride's enlightened criticism. Younger writers favorable to modern art emerged: Guy Pène du Bois, Forbes Watson, and the brilliant if dogmatic Willard Huntington Wright.

By the middle 1920's the modernists had won at least a partial victory. Not that they were universally accepted, but only in the most reactionary circles were they still considered lunatics and charlatans. A younger generation was arising to whom modernism was an accepted fact, and a point of departure for new developments.

MAX WEBER
Chinese Restaurant. 1915. Oil. 40 x 48.

Whitney Museum of American Art.

GEORGIA O'KEEFFE

From the Plains. 1919. Oil. 27 x 23.

Collection of Mr. and Mrs. Stephen A. Stone.

5 As the modern movements evolved in the United States, they produced fewer fundamental innovations than in Europe. To the Europeans, the resources of representational art appeared to be exhausted, and the only possible direction was the search for new concepts. So within a few years, European art passed through a series of revolutions. But our art had not yet reached this stage of development; up to 1913 it had been almost totally representational. Modernism here, at least in its early stages, was less a product of organic growth than of international influences. The United States was not yet the breeding ground of new concepts that Paris was; few new movements were born here. The achievements of American modernism were to be in personal expression on an individualistic plane, rather than basic innovations by movements and schools.

Some abstract art had been produced here before 1913, by either knowledgeable internationalists such as Weber or instinctive creators such as Dove. The Armory Show and its aftermath gave new impetus to abstraction, and for the next decade it was essayed by a dozen Americans. In general they were not doctrinaire; they formed no school, and their styles were personal and diversified. Much of their work was experimental and tentative, more often semi-abstract than pure abstract. Compared to the Europeans, they were concerned less with the exploration of fundamental form than with the expression of emotions and ideas in a visual language paralleling music.

Cubism had a few exponents, including Weber, Zorach, Dasburg and McFee; and in a highly personal romantic style, Arthur B. Davies, who arrayed his visionary figures of women in multicolored cubistic patterns. Its most lucid champion, not only in his work but in his writing and teaching, was Andrew Dasburg. Concentrating austerely on the geometric structure of objects and figures, he showed a preoccupation with basic form unusual among Americans, even when he abandoned abstraction for representation. But while cubism had few orthodox followers, its emphasis on three-dimensional volume and on design, and its tendency toward abstraction, had a definite effect on artists of other modernist persuasions.

But in general, American abstraction tended to be expressionist rather than formal — a characteristic that has continued to the present day. Its most inventive early practitioner, Max Weber, in his 1912 to 1916 phase was allied to cubism, but with a difference. His poetic interpretations of New York were cubistic in style, but their content, a rapturous response to the spectacle of the modern city, was closer to futurism and to Robert Delaunay's lyrics of Paris. By contrast with the

GEORGIA O'KEEFFE
Black Spot, Number 2. 1919. Oil. 24 x 16.

Collection of Mr. and Mrs. Irving Levick.

JOSEPH STELLA

Der Rosenkavalier. c.1915. Oil. 24 x 30.

Whitney Museum of American Art, gift of George F. Of.

JOSEPH STELLA

The Gas Tank. 1918. Oil. 40½ x 30.

Collection of Mr. and Mrs. Roy R. Neuberger.

austerity of analytical cubism, Weber expressed subjective emotions in a free chromatic style, with opulent color and curvilinear forms. His art, like that of his fellow pioneer in abstraction, Abraham Walkowitz, was also akin to Kandinsky's abstract expressionism.

Whether this affinity to Kandinsky, revealed by certain other Americans, was due to contact with his work, to their mutual Russian background, or simply to parallel development, is uncertain. But with Marsden Hartley the contact was direct: during three years in Germany between 1912 and 1915 he became affiliated with the *Blaue Reiter* group, of which Kandinsky was a leader, and under their liberating influence painted bold abstract compositions, powerful in their primary colors, superb in decorative values. Highly aware of other art, Hartley was to pass through less exuberant forms of abstraction before returning to representation about 1920.

Several Americans who remained abroad were involved in the European trend toward abstraction. The most eminent, Lyonel Feininger, in 1912 began working in a style generally cubist but with futurist overtones in its dynamism and pronounced lines of direction. His mature work was wider in content than early cubism, taking in elements of imagery, space, light, color, and romantic emotion that cubism shunned. Feininger himself said that his lifelong love of ships, locomotives and tall buildings began in his childhood and youth in Manhattan. His enhanced variation of cubism was curiously parallel to the native precisionism of Charles Demuth and Preston Dickinson.

In Paris, Morgan Russell and Stanton Macdonald-Wright launched their own abstract movement in 1913. Synchromism (meaning "with color") was a rival of Delaunay's Orphism, which in turn had been a revolt against cubism's monochromatic austerity. The two Americans, both intelligent theorists, went beyond Orphism in analyzing the relation of color to form: the fact that the warm colors appear to advance toward the eye and the cool ones to retreat, and that these sensations of projection and recession can be used to create form and space. The Synchromists engaged in a lively verbal battle with the Orphists, but actually their early compositions were much like their rivals': multicolored prisms and whirling disks. In the next few years they developed more complex and interesting designs — only to return shortly thereafter to representation. But their analysis of color-form relations, as enunciated by Macdonald-Wright's brother Willard Huntington Wright, had been a contribution to the aesthetics of abstraction, and their theories had influenced other Americans in Paris, including Thomas H. Benton, then struggling to reconcile Renaissance form with Synchromist color.

In Paris also, but allied to the Orphists, Patrick Henry Bruce continued faithful to abstraction into the 1930's. His early pure abstract compositions gave way to

C H A R L E S   D E M U T H
Modern Conveniences. 1921. Oil. 25$\frac{7}{16}$ x 20$\frac{15}{16}$.

The Columbus Gallery of Fine Arts, Ferdinand Howald Collection.

works with recognizable shapes, but his style remained uncompromising in its clarity, angular geometric forms, and strong pure color. Every picture was thoughtfully designed and solidly built, with a sense of architectonic structure unusual among his fellow countrymen.

In America, indigenous abstraction appeared in the work of Arthur G. Dove and Georgia O'Keeffe. The former's year and a half in France was spent mostly away from Paris, painting landscape, and only after his return to America did his individuality assert itself in an art close to the earth, with motifs derived from nature, transformed into strong rhythmic patterns and resonant color harmonies. He was one of the first Americans to paint pure abstractions, in a series of small oils as early as 1910, strangely parallel to Kandinsky but with no known influence.

From the beginning Georgia O'Keeffe's art was a personal language, without discernible derivations; growing out of nature, yet attaining abstraction as pure as music. In her remarkable abstract creations from the late 1910's on, the concepts were completely original, the design daring and effective, the style absolutely clearcut, yet always with a sense of enigmatic depths.

In the United States early abstraction as a movement lasted only until about 1920. After that, most of its exponents returned to more representational modes. This relatively short life can be attributed to several factors. Over here abstraction was not, as in Europe, the end product of historical evolution; it had no deep roots in the American past. Our art world, only recently emerged from impressionism, was not yet prepared for so complete a break with representation. The abstract movement had been the creation of young artists, many of them fresh from European experience and the stimulus of the Armory Show. As they grew older, most of them were attracted back to representational art, with its wealth of associative values. From the early 1920's to the middle 1930's only a few painters and sculptors in this country worked in abstract terms, and even they not exclusively: Dove, O'Keeffe, Carles, Stuart Davis, and younger men such as Gorky, Calder and Noguchi. Not until after 1935 did the second wave of abstraction begin to rise — the wave which is still running in full strength.

The United States of 1913, building its skyscrapers and automobiles and giant factories, could be called the most futurist nation. But its dynamism had produced no echo in academic art. The machine age had first found a voice in Italian futurism, Russian constructivism, and French and Spanish cubism, but not so far in the established art of America. New York, our most spectacular city, had been painted by a few mild impressionists and by the Henri group, who had pictured its human inhabitants. But about 1912 the city itself — the towering buildings, the great bridges, the flow of traffic, the kaleidoscope of Broadway at night — became

CHARLES SHEELER
Church Street El. 1920. Oil. 16 x 18½.

Collection of Mrs. Earle Horter.

CHARLES SHEELER
Pertaining to Yachts and Yachting. 1922. Oil. 20 x 24.

Philadelphia Museum of Art.

themes for the modernists, especially Marin, Weber, Walkowitz and Stella. Interpreting the city not by literal representation but in semi-abstract terms, they were the first to express in modern language the essential energies of machine-age America. In Marin's often-quoted words: "I see great forces at work, great movements . . . I can hear the sound of their strife, and there is great music being played."

But curiously enough, orthodox futurism found little following here. Launched in Italy in 1910 in reaction against cubism's limitations in subject and emotional content, it was a glorification of the machine, speed and dynamism: a doctrine which one might expect would appeal particularly to Americans. But due to the futurists' abstention from the Armory Show, they were not seen here as a group until the San Francisco Exposition of 1915; and thereafter they were seldom represented in our art world. The school had only one out-and-out American exponent, but an important one — Joseph Stella. Born in Italy, living in America since the 1890's, he had already been enraptured by the steel mills of Pittsburgh before he revisited his native land about 1909. Three years later, in Paris, he met the Italian futurist leaders. "When in 1912 I came back to New York," he wrote later, "I was thrilled to find America so rich with so many motives to be translated into a new art." Soon after the Armory Show he embarked on a series of big futurist fantasies based on New York — still among the most extraordinary imaginative syntheses of the modern city.

Though cubism, like futurism, had only a few adherents, its influence was much wider than its practice. Its concentration on form more than on color, its geometric character, its precision and sense of order, affected artists who did not follow it into abstraction. In particular, the painters who have been called precisionists, such as Demuth, Schamberg, Sheeler and Preston Dickinson, profited by the lessons of cubism. These men used the phenomena of urban and industrialized America — skyscrapers, factories, machine-made objects, and machines themselves — as raw material for their art. Though most of them were representational, they were concerned primarily with the geometric forms of such objects, and their translation into precise, ordered design.

Charles Demuth's early watercolors had revealed him as a subtle, sophisticated observer of society, a master of the medium, with a highly developed sense of decorative values. About 1919 he began to paint architectural motifs, in tempera and oil and on a larger scale, in a modified cubistic style. His art became an inventive play with the geometric, achieving design that combined nervous energy, extreme refinement, purity of form, and a classic sense of order. Similarly, Preston Dickinson translated the modern industrialized scene into precise linear patterns that recalled the Japanese printmakers. Morton Schamberg was one of the first Americans to explore the aesthetic possibilities of the machine, transforming its functional shapes into semi-abstract design of absolute clarity and precision, with a fine sense of the formal relations of part to part. A gifted artist, his promise was cut short by his early death. Charles Sheeler, thoroughly familiar with advanced art, especially cubism, at first experimented with semi-abstraction, then concentrated on the geometric forms of actual objects and buildings, achieving a synthesis of visual naturalism and strong, exactly planned formal structure.

The full development of precisionism took place after 1920 and involved many other artists; but one of its main sources was cubism's exploration of basic forms in the preceding decade. Paradoxically, Parisian cubism stimulated American painters to throw off impressionist softness and vagueness, and to return to the clarity that had marked precise realism in America, from Copley to Harnett.

Modernism's revolution in the language of art was paralleled by a revolution in imagery. Fauvism and cubism had freed art from the literal vision; Dada and surrealism were to free imagery from its limitation to external facts. The hidden world of the subconscious mind, explored by psycho-analysis, added its wealth of content to the objective facts of the "real" world. This exploration of the subconscious mind had begun early in the modern movement. Then came the World War with all its horrors, and its aftermath of disillusion. The Dada movement of 1916 was a product of the war years. Aimed at the annihilation of all known values, it was primarily destructive, and much of its energy went into demonstrations and verbal assaults against the established order. But its very destructiveness carried seeds for the future; its anti-rationalism prepared the ground for the surrealist movement of the 1920's, the first systematic school based on the subconscious as material for art.

During the war Marcel Duchamp and Francis Picabia lived in New York, and there in 1915 they and the American Man Ray launched a proto-Dada movement, and later produced revolutionary works such as Duchamp's "readymades," Picabia's irrational machine images, and Man Ray's arresting abstractions and aerographs. Duchamp and Picabia left the United States in 1918; Man Ray settled in Paris in 1921, to take an active part in the Dada and surrealist movements

STANTON MACDONALD-WRIGHT

"Oriental." Synchromy in Blue-Green. 1918. Oil. 36 x 50.

Whitney Museum of American Art.

HUGO ROBUS
Brass Band. 1917-18. Oil. 26 x 32.

Collection of the artist.

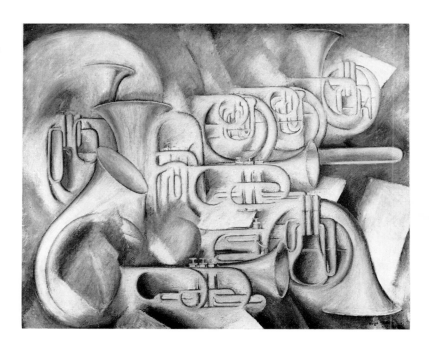

PRESTON DICKINSON
Industry, II. c.1920. Oil. 24¾ x 30.

Whitney Museum of American Art, gift of Mr. and Mrs. Alan H. Temple.

there; so the battlefield was transferred across the Atlantic. Dada had remained an exotic here; the United States had not suffered from the war as had Europe, nor did we have the weight of a great artistic past to combat. But the New York group's ideas and actual works were prophetic of certain advanced manifestations of today.

By far the most widespread form of modernism in America was to be expressionism. The word is a rather indefinite one, but the only one to describe one of the broadest tendencies in modern art. It had been first applied to the German modern schools such as *Die Brücke* and *Der Blaue Reiter,* which, reacting against impressionism's focus on the merely visual, turned to expression of subjective emotion. With time the word came to include the many varieties of modern art, neither naturalistic on the one hand nor abstract on the other, which aim to express emotion through imagery based on reality — but not realistically represented. Drawing on nature for motifs, expressionism uses her freely, translating her into pictorial images that tend toward abstraction or semi-abstraction. As John Marin wrote in 1916 of his own watercolors: "These works are meant as constructed expressions of the inner senses, responding to things seen and felt." Through rhythmic line, richness of substance, and above all through color, expressionism speaks to the senses, and through the senses to the emotions.

Expressionism proved particularly sympathetic to the American mind, which has never been drawn as much to purely aesthetic and formal qualities as to emotional expression based on reality. It was the American equivalent of fauvism, and the most widely practised mode among our pioneer modernists; and also the mode to which those who abandoned abstraction usually turned. Its currency can be ascribed in part to the emergence of many modernists of Central and Eastern European origin. Since the German expressionists were scantily represented in the Armory Show compared to the French moderns, and in the American art world for a good many years thereafter, it seems clear that expressionism here was less a product of foreign influence than a parallel development — a characteristic creation of the new America. To the sterility of established art it brought a new emotional freedom, a new sensuousness, and a more direct and moving visual language.

Expressionism was not so much a school as a broad tendency, highly diverse, with as many variations as there were individuals. To cite only a few: John Marin, one of the most instinctive of creators, with his lyrical interpretations of the electric vitality of New York, or the vibrant light of the Maine coast — works which embodied intense subjective emotion in dynamic pictorial design. Marsden Hartley's early mountain landscapes, whose visionary strangeness revealed his youthful admiration for Albert Ryder, and foretold his return to expressionism in later life.

MORTON L. SCHAMBERG

Mechanical Forms. Oil. 6½ x 4¾.

Collection of Mr. and Mrs. Roy R. Neuberger.

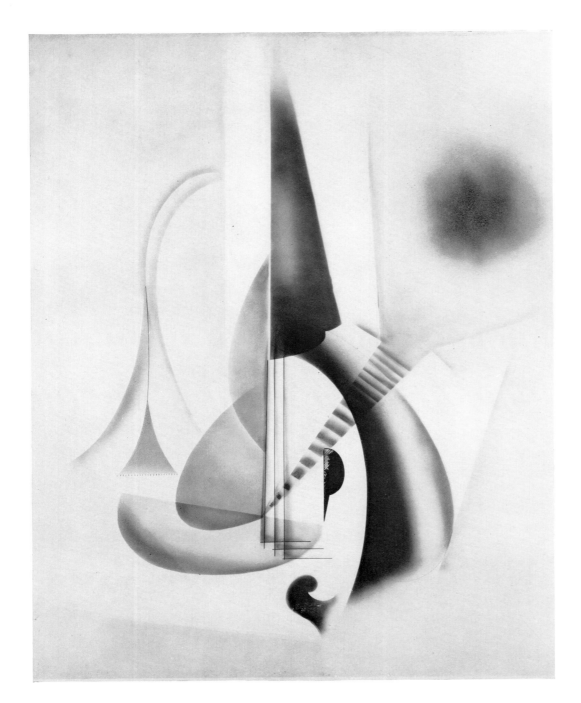

MAN RAY

Jazz. Air brush color. 31 x 25.

The Columbus Gallery of Fine Arts, Ferdinand Howald Collection.

Max Weber's art after he turned from abstraction: idyllic and religious themes, Biblical in spirit, pervaded by moods of serene contemplation or spiritual exaltation. Or the spontaneous expressionism of Charles Burchfield in his watercolors of 1916 to 1918: a personal nature poetry embodied in imagery as subjective as that of Van Gogh and the German expressionists, by a painter who had seen no modern European art.

American sculpture was touched by modernism much later and less than our painting. In the opening years of the century it was almost completely conservative. The neo-classic tradition had settled into a proficient academic art, coldly idealized, limited to naturalistic representation, a kind of three-dimensional photography. Historically, our sculptors had always been more conservative than our painters, and this held true well into the new century. There were few counterparts to the fauvist, cubist and expressionist painters. Since public commissions played a greater part, official backwardness weighed more heavily on sculptors. There were practical problems: the nature of the medium, solid and heavy, involving much work, and ample studio space. And there was American modernism's relative disregard of form, the basis of sculpture.

A few essays were made in sculptural abstraction: Max Weber's small pieces modeled in 1915 and 1917, among the earliest purely abstract sculpture produced anywhere; Robert Laurent's fluid semi-abstract wood carvings based on natural forms; and John Storrs' vigorous, massive constructions with their clearcut planes and pronounced angularity. But these innovations were few compared with the vital sculptural experimentation being carried on in Europe by Brancusi, Matisse, Duchamp-Villon, Picasso, Lipchitz and many others.

When the prevailing conservatism was interrupted it was by liberal rather than advanced sculptors. From the temporarily bankrupt classical tradition these men were drawn toward primitive, archaic or non-European art, embodying sculptural concepts free from academic naturalism and pseudo-classicism; especially African Negro sculpture, a revelation of uninhibited vitality.

The style of these sculptors was representational, but it was not naturalistic. Their most frequent theme was still the perennial one of the human (especially the female) figure, but they used it freely: details and literal proportions were disregarded, the dominant purpose was the creation of plastic form. They carved no frigid stone maidens. Gaston Lachaise's art was a hymn to the female and her sexual magnetism, incarnated in forms of the utmost amplitude, vitality and refinement: a sculptor in the great French tradition whose full creative career unfolded

MAX WEBER
Spiral Rhythm. 1915. Bronze. 24⅓″ high.

The Joseph H. Hirshhorn Collection.

JOHN STORRS
Abstract Sculpture. Bronze. 18" high.

The Downtown Gallery.

in this country. Elie Nadelman's witty images of society, suave and elegant in manner but with a severe purity of form; William Zorach's monumental simplicity and deep, healthy sensuousness; Robert Laurent's strong flowing rhythms and rich feeling for the material; and Maurice Sterne's concentration on powerful forms of archaic severity — with these artists American sculpture was awakening from barren neo-classicism into a new vitality. In the next two decades it was to grow constantly in creativity and inventiveness, introducing concepts of sculptural form and function even more revolutionary than in our painting.

6   By the early 1920's the momentum of the modern movements in the United States had begun to slow down. Culturally and politically, the new decade was one of reaction against the internationalism of the World War period, toward growing isolationism. On the positive side, it was a decade of the rediscovery of America, still a dark continent for the contemporary artist. The interest in the American scene, initiated by the Henri group and focused primarily on the Eastern cities, spread westward. In the Midwest appeared an articulate regionalist school, violently opposed to modernism's international and abstract tendencies. Then came the Depression, and the rise of an equally articulate social school, for which art without social content was mere formalism and decoration. These successive movements dominated the American art world from the middle 1920's to the later 1930's. In these years little advanced art existed in this country compared to Europe, and its few adherents were like members of an underground movement. Not until the late 1930's did the tide begin to turn.

This second wave of advanced art, which was predominantly abstract, met with quite a different reception than its predecessor. In Europe, innovation had never stopped; abstract art was almost two generations old, its historical validity had been recognized, its principles accepted, its laws formulated. In America, a younger generation was ready for it. Hence within a few years the second advanced movement achieved a dominance that the first had never approached.

By contrast, the modernists of the 1900's and 1910's had been pioneers in hostile territory. Contemporaries of the European founders of modernism, they had introduced the new art to a nation unprepared for it. There were not many of them, and they were relatively isolated. Neither members nor leaders of groups, they founded no schools and had few followers. By and large, they were individualists, working out their artistic destinies in an unresponsive environment.

ROBERT LAURENT
Head (Abstraction). 1916. Mahogany. 15″ high.

Collection of the artist.

MAURICE STERNE
The Bomb Thrower. 1910-14. Bronze. 12″ high.

Whitney Museum of American Art,
bequest of Mrs. Sam A. Lewisohn.

As we have seen, they produced few new basic concepts, no innovations as radical as those of Matisse and Picasso. Their achievements were in the field of personal expression, in the development of individual viewpoints and styles, rather than in launching new movements. The proportions of foreign influence and native originality varied with each. Most of them were affected by international modernism, but in differing ways and degrees. One might cite Marin as an example of the instinctive artist to whom modernism was a liberating atmosphere rather than a determining influence, and who realized himself in a highly personal style almost from the beginning; while Weber could stand for the knowledgeable artist, aware of current developments and experimenting with them, before going on to evolve his own mature artistic character. In both cases, it was what came from within, and what the artist made of what came from without, that counted in the end.

It was not necessarily those who were most advanced who created the most vital work. Only a few went as far as out-and-out abstraction; in general, no further than semi-abstraction or expressionism. Most of them maintained a base in the material of the "real" world, which they used with more or less freedom. But all of them, whether abstract, semi-abstract, expressionist, futurist, or precisionist, shared the fundamental conception of art as creation in the direct physical language of form and color, not as naturalistic representation — in which they differed basically from the academic mind.

In the advanced modes they made definite and lasting contributions: Weber's cubist-futurist inventions, Feininger's dynamic cubism, Hartley's abstract expressionism (his most powerful early work), Stella's Americanized futurism, Dove's and O'Keeffe's native abstractionism. But even in these advanced manifestations, some of the most vital were individual and unorthodox, owing little to current schools. And other artists less advanced created art equally valid: Prendergast's lyrical fauvism, Marin's intensely personal expressionism, Demuth's and Sheeler's precisionism, Lachaise's and Nadelman's revitalized classicism. Whether advanced or less advanced, these artists were authentic creators, expressing themselves in individual forms that were new. Seen in relation to today's abstract art, with its boldness, physical force, large scale, and revolutionary techniques, some of their work may now appear tentative in conception, restrained in form, quiet in color, modest in scale. But in the essential qualities of form and design, which outlast changes in style, the best of their work belongs among the most fully realized art created in America in our century.

The pioneer modernists of the 1900's and 1910's effected a revolution in our

GASTON LACHAISE
Walking Woman. 1922. Bronze. 19″ high.

The Joseph H. Hirshhorn Collection.

fundamental concepts of the nature of art. Instead of art as representation, they established the concept of art as independent creation in form and color. They restored to art its basis in the senses, its physical integrity. By discarding representation that had no plastic value, they purified art of much that was not art. And in freeing subject matter from naturalistic limitations, they opened up a new world of imagery. Even artists who did not adopt modernism benefitted by it. As John Sloan said, modern art was "a medicine for the disease of representing appearances." It was in no small part due to the modern movements that there has been for the past half-century in America a vital tradition of non-academic representational art, fully conscious of the "abstract" elements of design, though conceiving them differently.

Modernism was not only a revolution in the language of art; it was the visual expression of a new spirit, challenging the outworn Puritanism of established American culture at the turn of the century. It was an affirmative response to the modern world of the machine and the city. It was a freeing of emotional expression from genteel inhibitions. It brought a recognition of sex as a motivating power in all human affairs. It was a return to the physical and sensual springs of being. Thus the liberating influence of international modernism added its impetus to the vast forces in all fields that were transforming the America of fifty years ago to the vital and creative America of today.

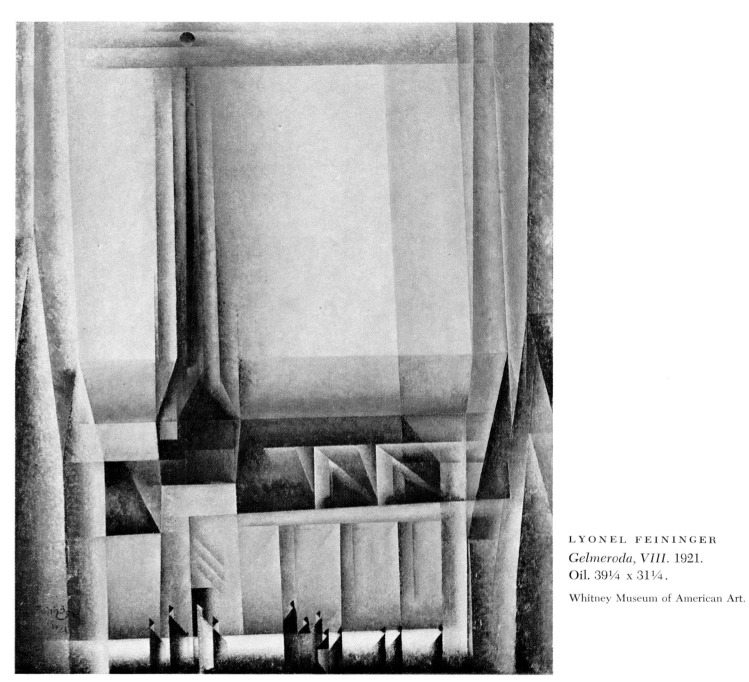

LYONEL FEININGER
Gelmeroda, VIII. 1921.
Oil. 39¼ x 31¼.

Whitney Museum of American Art.

GASTON LACHAISE
Nude Ascending.
1918. Marble. 29⅜ x 20.

[71]   Estate of Isabel Lachaise.

ELIE NADELMAN
Man in the Open Air. c.1915. Bronze. 54½″ high.

Collection, The Museum of Modern Art, New York, gift of William S. Paley.

ELIE NADELMAN

Tango. 1918. Polychromed wood. 34″ high.

Collection of Mrs. Edith Gregor Halpert.

JOHN MARIN

Manhattan, St. Paul's. 1914. Watercolor. 15 x 18¾.

The Metropolitan Museum of Art, The Alfred Stieglitz Collection.

CHARLES DEMUTH
End of the Parade: Coatesville, Pa. 1920. Tempera. 19½ x 15½.

Collection of Mrs. William Carlos Williams.

JOSEPH STELLA *Brooklyn Bridge.* 1917-1918. Oil. 84 x 76.

Yale University Art Gallery, Collection of the Société Anonyme.

JOSEPH STELLA
The Bridge. (One of five panels
of *New York Interpreted.*)
1920-1922. 88¼ x 54.

The Newark Museum.

MAX WEBER

Rush Hour, New York. 1915. Oil. 36¼ x 30¼.

Estate of Max Weber. Courtesy of the Downtown Gallery.

LYONEL FEININGER

Zirkow VII. 1918. Oil. 31½ x 39½.

Collection of Mrs. Julia Feininger.

MORRIS KANTOR
Orchestra. 1923. Oil. 35 x 34.

Collection of Mr. and Mrs. Edgar B. Miller.

GEORGIA O'KEEFFE
Music, Pink and Blue, Number 2. 1919. Oil. 35½ x 29.

Collection of the artist.

ALFRED H. MAURER

Abstraction: Fishing. c.1919. Oil. 21¾ x 18.

Courtesy of Hudson D. Walker.

STUART DAVIS
The President. 1917. Oil. 36 x 26.

The Downtown Gallery.

A LA FORME. ORANGE.

MORGAN RUSSELL
Synchromy to Form: Orange. 1913-1914. Oil. 135 x 123.

Albright-Knox Art Gallery, gift of Seymour H. Knox.

PATRICK HENRY BRUCE
Still Life. c.1920. Oil. 23¾ x 28¾.

Collection of Mr. and Mrs. Roy R. Neuberger.

PATRICK HENRY BRUCE
Composition I. c.1918. Oil. 45½ x 34¾.

Yale University Art Gallery, Collection of the Société Anonyme.

[85]

MORTON L. SCHAMBERG
Machine. 1916. Oil. 30⅛ x 22¾.

Yale University Art Gallery, Collection of the Société Anonyme.

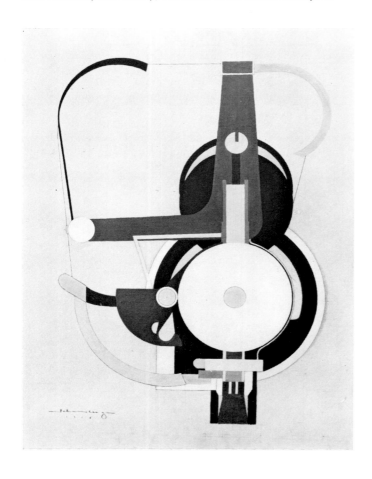

JOHN COVERT
Vocalization. 1919.

Oil and wooden dowels on composition board. 23¾ x 26½.

Yale University Art Gallery, Collection of the Société Anonyme.

MAN RAY

The Rope Dancer Accompanies Herself with Her Shadows. 1916. Oil. 52 x 73⅜.

Collection, The Museum of Modern Art, New York, gift of G. David Thompson.

The Rope Dancer Accompanies Herself With Her Shadows

BIOGRAPHICAL NOTES

BY EDWARD BRYANT

These biographical notes cover the artists referred to or illustrated in this book; they do not include all the early American modernists.

The following were represented in the Armory Show: Bluemner, Bruce, Burlin, Carles, Dasburg, Davies, Davis, Duchamp, Halpert, Hartley, Karfiol, Kuhn, Lachaise, Marin, Maurer, Nadelman, Pach, Pascin, Prendergast, Russell, Schamberg, Sheeler, Stella, Walkowitz, Marguerite Zorach and William Zorach.

The "Younger American Painters" exhibition in Alfred Stieglitz's gallery, 291 Fifth Avenue, March 1910, included Carles, Dove, Hartley, Marin, Maurer, Steichen and Weber.

The "Forum Exhibition of Modern American Painters" at the Anderson Galleries, New York, March 1916 — an important exhibition with an illustrated catalogue containing statements by the artists — included Benn, Bluemner, Dasburg, Dove, Hartley, Macdonald-Wright, Marin, Maurer, McFee, Man Ray, Russell, Sheeler, Walkowitz, Marguerite Zorach and William Zorach.

Abbreviations: ASL — Art Students League of New York. MOMA — Museum of Modern Art, New York. NAD — National Academy of Design, New York. PAFA — Pennsylvania Academy of the Fine Arts, Philadelphia. WMAA — Whitney Museum of American Art.

A. S. BAYLINSON. Born Moscow, 1882. To America with family as a boy. Studied NAD; with Henri at Chase School; later with Homer Boss. After 1913, strongly influenced by cubism; during 1920's progressively less geometric style. First one-man show, Little Book Store, N. Y., 1924. Secretary of Society of Independent Artists, 1917-34. Fire destroyed almost all of twenty years' work, 1931. Taught ASL, 1931-33; 1937-38. Died New York, 1950. Memorial exhibition, ASL, 1951.

BEN BENN. Born Russia, 1884. Brought up in New York. Studied NAD, 1904-08. First exhibited with other advanced artists in group shows in New York from 1912. First one-man show, J. B. Neumann's New Art Circle, N. Y., 1925. Work developed from fauvist style, c. 1915, to cubist-influenced "symbolic" portraits and landscapes, late 1910's and 1920's. Freer calligraphic organization in later works. Retrospective exhibition, Walker Art Center, Minneapolis, 1953. Lives in New York.

ALBERT BLOCH. Born St. Louis, 1882. Educated in St. Louis and New York. In 1908 to Germany for thirteen years. In Munich was associated with *Der Blaue Reiter* group from their first exhibition, 1911, and participated in all their group shows; also exhibited with *Der Sturm,* Berlin, 1914-17, and in other significant European shows; close association with Marc, Kandinsky, Klee, Campendonk. Returned to U. S. 1921. Taught Chicago Academy of Fine Arts, 1922; University of Kansas, 1923-47. Retrospective exhibition there, 1955. Died Lawrence, Kansas, 1961.

OSCAR BLUEMNER. Born Hanover, Germany, 1867. Studied painting and architecture, Germany. First one-man show at eighteen, Berlin. To America 1892; became successful architect. In 1912 turned entirely to painting. To Europe 1912-13. Impressed by German expressionism and cubism. One-man show, "291", 1915; exhibited there regularly until 1928. Died South Braintree, Mass., 1938. Retrospective exhibition, University of Minnesota, 1939.

PATRICK HENRY BRUCE. Born Richmond, Virginia, 1881. Studied with Henri, 1902-03. Settled in Paris c. 1906. Exhibited Salon d'Automne 1907-10. Among original group in Matisse class, 1908. Early post-impressionist style influenced by Cézanne and Renoir. Later, c. 1913, was associated with Delaunay and the Orphists; period of pure abstractions, c. 1914-18. First one-man show, Montross Gallery, N. Y., 1916. After early 1920's, work rarely seen; destroyed many canvases. Remained in Paris until shortly before his death in New York, 1937.

CHARLES BURCHFIELD. Born Ashtabula Harbor, Ohio, 1893. Has spent his life in eastern Ohio and western New York State. Studied Cleveland School of Art (Keller, Wilcox, Eastman). In New York for short period, 1916. First exhibition, Mrs. Mary Mowbray-Clarke's Sunwise Turn Bookshop, N. Y., 1916. Expressionist watercolors based on childhood memories, 1916-18. During 1920's realistic portrayals of the American small town. Since 1943, imaginative interpretations of nature themes. Member National Institute and Academy of Arts and Letters. Retrospective exhibitions: Carnegie Institute, Pittsburgh, 1938; Albright Art Gallery, Buffalo, N. Y., 1941; Cleveland Museum of Art, 1953; WMAA, 1956. Lives in West Seneca, N. Y.

PAUL BURLIN. Born New York, 1886. Educated in England. Illustrator, New York, 1903. Short trip to Italy and Brittany c. 1908. First one-man show, Daniel Gallery, N. Y., 1913. In New Mexico 1913-20; deeply interested in Indian and ancient American art. Paris, 1921-32; friend of Albert Gleizes and Leo Stein. Traveled throughout Europe and to North Africa. One-man show, Berlin, 1927. His expressionist style during 1930's tended toward social-realism; in 1940's, violent distortions and strong color; since 1950's related to abstract expressionism. Retrospective exhibition circulated by American Federation of Arts, 1962. Lives in New York.

ARTHUR B. CARLES. Born Philadelphia, 1882. Studied PAFA, 1901, 1903-07. Paris, 1905, 1907-12, 1920, 1929. Fauve style influenced by Matisse, c. 1910. In 1920's evolved decorative representational style, richly colored, sometimes semi-abstract; during 1930's painted more abstractly. Taught PAFA, 1917-25. Died Chestnut Hill, Pa., 1952. Retrospective exhibitions: Philadelphia Museum, 1946; PAFA and Philadelphia Museum, 1953.

JOHN COVERT. Born Pittsburgh, 1882. Studied Pittsburgh School of Design. In Munich, 1908-12. Paris, 1912-14; exhibited Salon, 1914. Traveled in England and through Europe. Returned to U. S. 1916. A founder and director of Society of Independent Artists, 1917. Developed highly individual construc-

tivist style, 1915-23. In 1923 gave up painting for business; after successful career in steel industry, retired in 1949 and returned to New York, living in seclusion until his death in 1960.

KONRAD CRAMER. Born Würzburg, Germany, 1888. Studied Academy of Fine Arts, Karlsruhe, under Thoma and Trübner. His modern tendencies first stimulated by *Der Blaue Reiter* group in Munich. Came to America, 1911, and settled in Woodstock, N. Y. Exhibited at MacDowell Club, N. Y., 1913. Member of "291" and friend of Alfred Stieglitz. Also a photographer. Founded Woodstock School of Photography, 1936. Died Woodstock, 1963.

ANDREW DASBURG. Born Paris, 1887. Came to U. S. 1892. Studied ASL (Cox and Du Mond); with Henri, 1902; and with Birge Harrison three summers at Woodstock, N. Y. Paris, 1909-10. Influenced by Cézanne. In Paris and London, 1914. Taught ASL, 1919-20. First one-man show, Rehn Gallery, N. Y., 1928. Visits to Taos, N. M., from 1916; resident there since 1930. Retrospective exhibition circulated by American Federation of Arts, 1959.

ARTHUR B. DAVIES. Born Utica, N. Y., 1862. To Chicago 1878; studied Chicago Academy of Design (Robertson); Art Institute of Chicago (Corwin). To New York 1886. Studied Gotham Art Students and ASL. First trip to Europe 1893. First one-man show, Macbeth Gallery, N. Y., 1896. To California 1905. In "The Eight" exhibition, Macbeth Gallery, N. Y., 1908. As president of the Association of American Painters and Sculptors, 1912-13, he was a key figure in organizing the Armory Show. Turned briefly to cubism c. 1915 but soon reverted to romantic style. Assisted new artists, and acted as advisor to prominent collectors. Died in Italy, 1928. Retrospective exhibitions: Metropolitan Museum of Art, 1930; Munson-Williams-Proctor Institute, Utica, 1962.

STUART DAVIS. Born Philadelphia, 1894. Studied with Henri, 1910-13. Illustrator for *The Masses*, 1913-16. First one-man show, Sheridan Square Gallery, N. Y., 1917. Made maps for Army Intelligence, 1918. After post-impressionist phase related to Van Gogh and the fauves, c. 1919, turned to abstract and semi-abstract painting, of which he has been one of chief American exponents. First trip abroad, Paris, 1928-29. Taught ASL, N. Y., 1931-32; New School for Social Research, N. Y., 1940-50. Member National Institute of Arts and Letters. Guggenheim International Award, 1960. Major retrospective exhibitions: MOMA, 1945; Walker Art Center, Minneapolis, and WMAA, 1957. Lives in New York.

CHARLES DEMUTH. Born Lancaster, Pa., 1883. Studied PAFA (Anshutz, Chase, Breckenridge, McCarter), 1905-10. First trip to Europe (Paris, London, Berlin), 1907. In Paris 1912-14; studied Académies Colarossi, Moderne and Julian; associated with Marcel Duchamp. Early work mostly in watercolor, influenced by the fauves, Rodin drawings, Toulouse-Lautrec, Cézanne. About 1917 began architectural and industrial subjects, in tempera, then in oil. After 1914 spent most of life in Lancaster. First one-man show, Daniel Gallery, N. Y., 1915. Frequented "291"; close friend of Stieglitz and O'Keeffe; one-man shows at An American Place. Trips to Bermuda 1916-17; to Paris 1921. Died Lancaster, 1935. Retrospective exhibitions: WMAA, 1937; MOMA, 1950.

PRESTON DICKINSON. Born New York, 1891. Studied ASL. In Paris 1910-15. Work c. 1913 showed deep influence of Japanese printmakers; soon afterward strongly influenced by Cézanne. First exhibited 1921. First one-man show, Daniel Gallery, N. Y., 1924. Frequent trips to Canada and Europe. Died in Spain, 1930.

ARTHUR G. DOVE. Born Canandaigua, N. Y., 1880. Studied Hobart College; Cornell University. 1903-07, successful career as illustrator, which he renounced after trip to France and Italy, 1908-10; exhibited Salon d'Automne, 1908, 1909. Close friend of Maurer. By 1910 was working in abstract style, based on forms in nature rather than derived from cubism. First one-man show, 1912, at "291", where he exhibited regularly thereafter. Died Huntington, N. Y., 1946. Major retrospective exhibitions: Cornell University, 1954; University of California, Los Angeles, 1958.

MARCEL DUCHAMP. Born Blainville, France, 1887. Studied Académie Julian, Paris, 1904. Joined cubists, 1911. Exhibited Section d'Or, 1912. To New York 1915. Active in Dada movement with Picabia and Man Ray. Founding member of Society of Independent Artists, 1916. With Katherine S. Dreier, organized Société Anonyme, first museum of modern art, N. Y., 1920. Returned to Paris 1919. Associated with Dada and surrealist movements in Paris until 1925. From 1923 devoted himself to chess and experiments in optics. U. S. citizen 1955. Lives in New York. Retrospective exhibition with his brothers Jacques Villon and Raymond Duchamp-Villon, Guggenheim Museum, 1957.

LYONEL FEININGER. Born New York, 1871. To Germany 1887. Studied Kunstgewerbeschule, Hamburg, and Berlin Academy, 1887-89; Académie Colarossi, Paris, 1892. Illustrator and cartoonist for German, French and American periodicals, 1894-1907. Came under influence of cubism on visit to Paris, 1911. Exhibited with *Der Blaue Reiter* group, Munich, 1913. Taught at Bauhaus in Weimar and Dessau, 1919-33. Exhibited extensively in Germany, 1920-33; retrospective exhibition, National Gallery, Berlin, 1931. First show in U. S. at Anderson Gallery, N. Y., 1923. Returned to U. S. 1937. Major retrospective exhibitions: MOMA, 1944; San Francisco Museum of Art, 1959; Kunstverein, Hamburg, 1961. Died New York, 1956.

SAMUEL HALPERT. Born Bialostock, Russia, 1884. Came to America at five. Studied NAD (Beckwith), 1899-1902; Ecole des Beaux-Arts, Paris, 1902-03 (Léon Bonnat). Remained in Paris until World War I, traveling extensively, occasionally returning to U. S. Interested early in Cézanne and modernism; knew many leaders of modern movement in Europe; participated in modern exhibitions abroad. First one-man show in U. S., Daniel Gallery, N. Y., 1919. Head of Art School, Society of Arts and Crafts, Detroit, 1926-30. Died Detroit, 1930.

MARSDEN HARTLEY. Born Lewiston, Maine, 1877. Studied Cleveland School of Art (John Semon, Yates), 1892; Chase School, N. Y., (Chase, Du Mond, Mora), 1898-1900; and NAD, 1900-01. Summers in Maine, 1901-08. Early Segantini influence; "black mountain" series influenced by Ryder, 1909. First one-man show, "291", 1909. First of numerous trips abroad, 1912-13; Paris and Germany. Briefly interested in cubism, then turned to abstract compositions. Exhibited with *Der Blaue Reiter*, Munich, and first Herbstsalon, Berlin, 1913. Brief return to U. S. 1913; to Germany 1914-17. One-man show, Berlin, 1916. Gave up abstraction for expressionism c. 1919. Frequent trips to Europe and American Southwest, 1921-36. Lived in Aix-en-Provence 1926-28. Lived in Maine from 1937 until his death in Ellsworth, Maine, 1943. Major retrospective exhibitions: MOMA, 1944; Stedelijk Museum, Amsterdam, 1962.

MORRIS KANTOR. Born Minsk, Russia, 1896. Came to U. S. 1909. Studied Independent School of Art, N. Y. (Homer Boss). In France 1927. In early 1920's, strong influence of cubism and Duchamp; then evolved a realist style with surrealist overtones; and in recent years, abstraction. First one-man show, Rehn Gallery, N. Y., 1930. Has taught at Cooper Union and ASL. Lives in New City, N. Y.

BERNARD KARFIOL. Born Budapest, Hungary, 1886, of American parents. Childhood on Long Island. Studied NAD, 1900. To Paris 1901; studied Académie Julian (Jean Paul Laurens) and independently. Exhibited Paris Salon, 1904; Salon d'Automne, 1905. Knew Rousseau, Matisse and other modernist leaders. Travel throughout Europe. Return to U. S. c. 1907. Taught 1908-13; class in Mrs. Harry Payne Whitney's Eighth Street studio for two years. First one-man show, Ardsley Studio, Brooklyn, 1917. Summers at Ogunquit, Maine. Died Irvington-on-Hudson, N. Y., 1952.

WALT KUHN. Born New York, 1877. Cartoonist in San Francisco 1899-1900. Europe, 1901-04; studied Académie Colarossi, Paris, and Royal Academy, Munich. Taught New York School of Art, 1908. First one-man show, Madison Gallery, N. Y., 1910. He and Davies were the leading organizers of the Armory Show. Art advisor to John Quinn, 1912-20. Died White Plains, N. Y., 1949. Retrospective exhibition, Cincinnati Art Museum, 1960.

GASTON LACHAISE. Born Paris, 1882. Studied Ecole Bernard Palissy; Académie Nationale des Beaux-Arts. Worked for René Lalique, jewelry and glass designer, for a year. To U. S. 1906. Assistant to sculptor Henry H. Kitson, Boston, 1906-12. To New York 1912. First major work, *Standing Woman*, begun 1912. Became assistant to Paul Manship, 1913. First one-man show, Bourgeois Gallery, N. Y., 1918. Retrospective exhibition, MOMA, 1935. Died New York, 1935.

ROBERT LAURENT. Born Concarneau, Brittany, 1890. Came to U. S. at eleven. Studied with Hamilton Easter Field. Paris, 1906-07; Rome, 1908-09, working with woodcarver Doratori. Became interested in African sculpture in Paris; was in touch with modern movement and its leaders here and abroad. Worked mostly in wood until 1918. Joint exhibition with Field, Daniel Gallery, N. Y., 1915. Taught University of Indiana, 1942-61; retrospective exhibition there, 1961. Lives in Bloomington, Indiana.

STANTON MACDONALD-WRIGHT. Born Charlottesville, Va., 1890. In France 1907-16. Studied in Paris at Ecole des Beaux-Arts, Académie Colarossi, and Sorbonne. Exhibited Salon d'Automne, 1910. In 1913 he and Morgan Russell formulated Synchromism. In 1913 exhibited in first Synchromist presentations, Carroll Gallery, N. Y., and in Paris and Munich. Returned to New York 1916. First one-man show, "291", 1917. Returned to figurative style c. 1919, but in recent years has worked in non-objective style. Did not exhibit 1919-32. Settled in California in early 1920's. Has since made intensive studies in Oriental art. Retrospective exhibition, Los Angeles County Museum, 1956. Lives at Pacific Palisades, Cal.

HENRY LEE McFEE. Born in St. Louis, 1886. Settled in Woodstock, N. Y., 1908; studied in summer classes ASL (Birge Harrison). Became interested in modern movement, especially Cézanne and the cubists, c. 1911. Exhibited at MacDowell Club, N. Y., 1912. First trip to Europe 1921. After a cubist phase, turned to a more naturalistic style in mid-1920's. From 1942 taught at Scripps College, Claremont, Cal. Died Altadena, Cal., 1953.

JOHN MARIN. Born Rutherford, N. J., 1870. Trained and practised as an architect. Studied painting at PAFA, 1899-1901; ASL, 1901-03. To Europe, 1905-09, 1910-11. First one-man show, "291", 1909; closely associated with Stieglitz the rest of his life. Member National Institute and Academy of Arts and Letters. Lived Cliffside, N. J., from 1916. Summers in Maine, where he died at Cape Split, 1953. Major retrospective exhibitions: MOMA, 1936; Institute of Modern Art, Boston, 1947; University of California, Los Angeles, 1956; Corcoran Gallery of Art, 1962; University of Arizona, 1963.

ALFRED MAURER. Born New York, 1868, son of Louis Maurer, Currier & Ives artist. Worked in family lithographic firm; studied NAD (Ward), 1884. Became successful academic painter, winning first prize, Carnegie International, 1901. To Europe 1897; studied briefly at Académie Julian. Friend of Gertrude Stein and Matisse. Began painting in a fauvist style c. 1907-08; later, cubist-abstraction and fantasy. First one-man show in New York, "291", 1909. Returned to America 1914. Died New York, 1932. Retrospective exhibition, Walker Art Center, Minneapolis, and WMAA, 1949.

ELIE NADELMAN. Born Warsaw, 1882. Studied Warsaw and Munich, and independently in Paris where he lived for twelve years. One-man shows, Paris, 1909, 1913; London, 1911. Patronage of Madame Helena Rubinstein from 1911. To America 1914. First New York one-man show, "291", 1915. Collector of folk art. After 1929 lived in seclusion, continuing to work. Died in New York, 1946. Memorial exhibition, MOMA, 1948.

GEORGIA O'KEEFFE. Born Sun Prairie, Wisconsin, 1887. Studied Art Institute of Chicago (Vanderpoel), 1904-05; ASL (Chase, Mora), 1907; Columbia University (Arthur Dow, Alan Bement), 1914-16. Freelance commercial artist, Chicago, 1909-10. From 1912-16 taught art in Texas, University of Virginia, and Columbia College, S. C. First abstract work, 1915. First one-man show, "291", 1916. Married Alfred Stieglitz, 1924. Retrospective exhibitions: Art Institute of Chicago, 1943; MOMA, 1946; Dallas Museum of Fine Arts, 1953; Worcester Museum of

Art, 1960. Member National Institute and Academy of Arts and Letters. Has traveled widely but did not go to Europe until after her style had fully developed. Lives in Abiquiu, N. M.

WALTER PACH. Born New York, 1883. Studied with Henri and in Chase's European summer classes. In Paris 1904, 1905, 1907-08, 1910-13. Closely identified with modern movement both as painter and critic. Active in selecting European section of Armory Show and handling its sales and publicity. One of chief organizers of the Society of Independent Artists, 1916. Wrote first article on Cézanne to appear in America, many art books, and translated Elie Faure and Delacroix's *Journals.* Taught at Columbia and New York Universities. Died New York, 1958.

JULES PASCIN. Born Vidin, Bulgaria, 1885. Began as illustrator in Munich, 1903. To Paris 1905. First one-man show, Martin Birnbaum's Berlin Photographic Company, N. Y., 1915. In U. S. 1914-20; became American citizen. Traveled extensively in U. S. and Cuba. An active member of the Penguin artist club. Influenced several American figure painters, including Karfiol, Brook, Ganso, Kuniyoshi. Returned to Paris 1920; visited U. S. 1927-28. Died Paris, 1930.

MAURICE PRENDERGAST. Born St. John's, Newfoundland, 1859. Brought up in Boston. Six trips to Europe before 1915, three before 1900. Studied Académies Julian and Colarossi, Paris, 1891-94. One-man show, Chase Gallery, Boston, 1897. To Italy 1898. First champion of Cézanne in America, and for several years a lone pioneer of modernism in this country. Influenced at first by Whistler and Manet, then by the Nabis, by Venetian art, and from c. 1909 by Signac. In "The Eight" exhibition, Macbeth Gallery, N. Y., 1908. The Armory Show brought him his first real recognition. Died New York, 1924. Retrospective exhibitions: WMAA, 1934; Addison Gallery of American Art, 1938; Museum of Fine Arts, Boston, 1960.

MAN RAY. Born Philadelphia, 1890. Turned from study of architecture and engineering to painting in 1907. Studied NAD 1908. First one-man show, Daniel Gallery, N. Y., 1915. Interest in abstract art began with Armory Show. Met Duchamp 1915. A founding member of Société Anonyme, 1920. Lived in Paris, 1921-40, turned to photography and cinema; principal American member of the Dada group; member of Surrealist movement, 1924-39. Lives in Paris. Retrospective exhibition, Princeton University, 1963.

HUGO ROBUS. Born Cleveland, 1885. Studied Cleveland School of Art (Potter), 1904-08; NAD, 1910-11. Europe, 1912-

14; studied sculpture with Bourdelle, Académie de la Grande Chaumière, Paris; traveled in southern France and Italy. Settled in New York 1915. Paintings after his return show strong cubist influence. Stopped painting and turned to sculpture, 1920. First one-man show, Grand Central Galleries, N. Y., 1946. Retrospective exhibition circulated by American Federation of Arts, 1960. Lives in New York.

MORGAN RUSSELL. Born New York, 1886. Studied with Henri 1906-07. Protégé of Mrs. Harry Payne Whitney, c. 1905-16. Went to Paris 1906. Studied with Matisse 1908-09. Friend of Modigliani. He and Macdonald-Wright founded the Synchromist movement, 1913. Exhibited Bernheim-Jeune Galleries, Paris, and in Munich, 1913; Indépendants, Paris, 1913, 1914. Returned to a figurative style c. 1920. Lived in France until 1946. Died Broomall, Pa., 1953.

MORTON L. SCHAMBERG. Born Philadelphia, 1882. Studied architecture, University of Pennsylvania, 1899-1903; painting, PAFA, 1903-04, 1905-06. To Europe with Chase's summer classes, 1902, 1903, 1904. To Paris 1906. Shared studio with Sheeler, Philadelphia, 1906-09. To Europe with Sheeler, 1908-09; first contact with modernism. Portrait photography c. 1913. Assembled Philadelphia's first exhibition of modern art, McClees Gallery, 1915. First influenced by Matisse and cubism, he became interested in machine subjects c. 1916, possibly influenced by Picabia and Duchamp. Died Philadelphia, 1918.

CHARLES SHEELER. Born Philadelphia, 1883. Studied School of Industrial Art, Philadelphia, 1900-03; PAFA (Chase), 1903-06. To Europe with Chase's summer classes, 1904, 1905; with Schamberg, 1908; with family, 1909. In Philadelphia 1910-19. Began professional photography 1912. Exhibited at de Zayas' Modern Gallery, N. Y., 1918 (photographs) and 1920 (paintings and photographs); at Daniel Gallery, N. Y., 1922 (paintings). Lived in New York 1919-27. Semi-abstract paintings in 1910's, followed in 1920's by precise realism and strong architectural organization. During 1940's style more geometric. Member of National Institute of Arts and Letters. Has lived in Irvington-on-Hudson, N. Y., since 1942. Major retrospective exhibitions: MOMA, 1939; University of California, Los Angeles, 1954; Allentown (Pa.) Art Museum, 1961; University of Iowa, 1963.

JOSEPH STELLA. Born Muro Lucano, Italy, prob. 1877. To New York 1896. Studied New York School of Art (Chase), 1902. Magazine illustrator, 1905-10; sent by *The Survey* to Pittsburgh to draw steel mills and workers. First contact with modern art while in Italy and France, 1909-12. Exhibited in Rome 1910. Met several of the Italian futurists but did not become futurist himself until return to U. S. First major futurist painting, *Battle of Lights, Coney Island*, begun 1913, exhibited at Montross Gallery, N. Y., 1914. Director of Society of Independent Artists, 1916. First one-man show, Bourgeois Gallery, N. Y., 1920. 1920-23, *New York Interpreted* series, now in Newark Museum. Retrospective exhibition, Newark Museum, 1939. Died New York, 1946.

MAURICE STERNE. Born Libau, Latvia, 1878. To New York 1889. Studied NAD 1894-99. First one-man show, Old Country Sketch Club, N. Y., 1902. Traveled in Europe 1904-08; in Paris came in early contact with the work of Cézanne and the modernists; to France, Germany, Italy, Greece, studying especially the early Italians. Exhibited Paul Cassierer Gallery, Berlin, 1910; Berlin Photographic Company, N. Y., 1912. To Egypt and the East 1911-12. In Bali, 1912-14, produced many paintings and drawings of native life. Traveled extensively thereafter. Retrospective exhibitions: MOMA, 1933; Phillips Collection, Washington, D. C., 1952. Died New York, 1957.

JOHN STORRS. Born Chicago, 1885. In 1907 to Germany to study art; traveled in Europe, Greece, Turkey, Egypt, 1907-08. Studied Boston and Philadelphia 1908-10. Paris, 1910-12; studied Académie Julian; and under Rodin, 1912-14. First one-man exhibition, Folsom Galleries, N. Y., 1920. Frequent trips between U. S. and Europe. Executed several architectural sculpture projects. Taught Art Institute of Chicago, 1930. Began to paint 1931. Lived in France from 1930's until his death in 1956.

ABRAHAM WALKOWITZ. Born Tumen, Siberia, 1880. To U. S. in early childhood. Studied NAD (Shirlaw); Académie Julian, Paris. To Europe, 1906-07, 1914, 1931, spending five years and traveling widely. First exhibited at Haas Gallery, N. Y., 1908; four shows at "291" between 1912 and 1917. Director and Vice President of Society of Independent Artists for 23 years. Lives in Brooklyn, N. Y.

MAX WEBER. Born Byelostock, Russia, 1881; grew up in Brooklyn. Studied Pratt Institute (Dow), 1898-1900. Taught art in Virginia and Minnesota, 1900-05. In Europe, 1905-08. Studied Académie Julian one season; visited Spain, Italy, Belgium and Holland. Exhibited Indépendants, 1906, 1907; Salon d'Automne, 1906. In the Matisse class, 1908. Returned to U. S. 1909; work became increasingly advanced. First one-man show, Haas Gallery, N. Y., 1909. First sculpture 1911. Invited by Roger Fry to Grafton Group exhibition, London, 1913, at time of Armory Show. One of earliest international exponents of abstract art, his work evolved from fauvism (1909-11) to an abstract style related to cubism and futurism (1912-19), changing c. 1920 to more representational subjects. Member National Institute of Arts and Letters. Died Great Neck, N. Y., 1961. Major retrospective exhibitions: MOMA, 1930; WMAA, 1949; Newark Museum, 1959; American Academy of Arts and Letters, 1962.

MARGUERITE ZORACH. Born Santa Rosa, Cal., 1887. To Paris, 1907, for four years; studied at La Palette. Impressed by fauve works at Salon d'Automne. Exhibited Paris Salon 1909; Salon d'Automne 1910, 1911. Returned to U. S. 1911. One-man show (with William Zorach, her husband), Daniel Gallery, N. Y., 1915. Also noted for her embroidered tapestries. Lives in Brooklyn, N. Y.

WILLIAM ZORACH. Born Eurburg, Lithuania, 1887. To America 1891. Brought up in Cleveland. Studied Cleveland School of Art 1903-06; NAD and ASL 1907-09. In France 1910-11; studied at La Palette (Jacques Emil Blanche); painted in Southern France. Exhibited Salon d'Automne 1911. First one-man show, Taylor Galleries, Cleveland, 1912. Paintings markedly fauve in character, 1913-16. In 1917 began to do sculpture, to which he devoted himself from 1922. Lecturer on sculpture, Columbia University, 1932-35; has taught sculpture ASL, 1929 to present. Member National Institute of Arts and Letters. Retrospective exhibition, WMAA, 1959. Lives in Brooklyn, N. Y.

INDEX The numerals in *italic* type refer to illustrations.

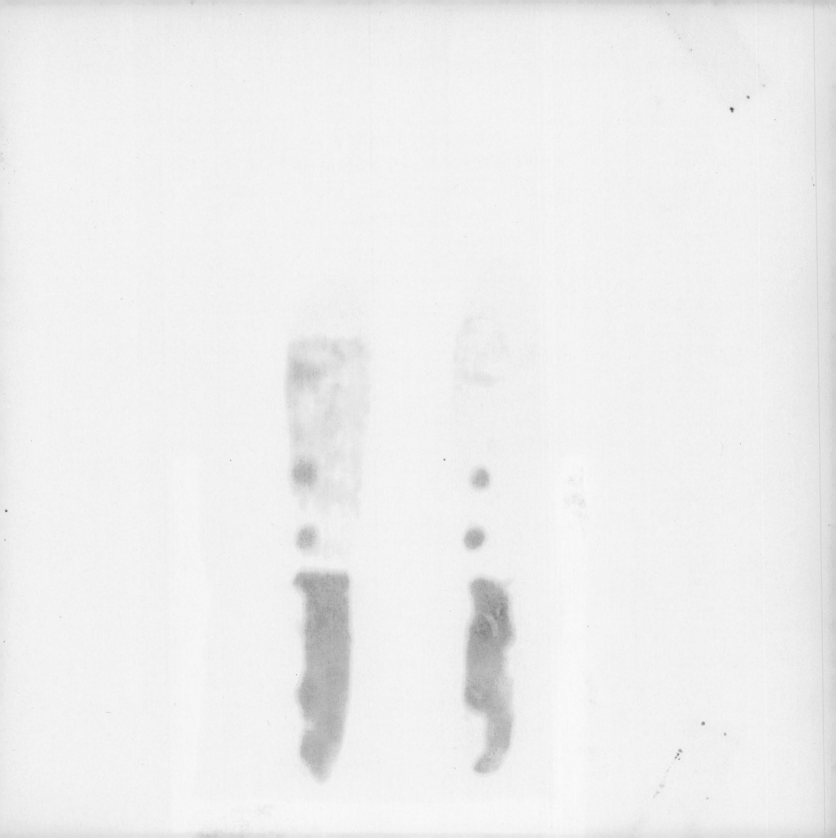

12/20/63